Puntification

No Pun Intended?

As Lewis Carroll said, "When I use a word, it means just what I choose it to mean—neither more nor less."

H. Dumpty, Esq.

Puntification
No Pun Intended?

By Milton B. Lederman, Ph.D.
(a.k.a. Attila the Pun)

Illustrations by Ray Rueby

Puntification
No Pun Intended?

ISBN   978-0-9740428-4-8
Published by Tobey Arts
ruebyr@frontiernet.net
Pittsford, NY 14534

First Edition

*To the memory of my kid brother
Irving H. Lederman, with whom I
often traded jokes and always shared
infinite affection.*

About The Author ~

Milton B. Lederman was born in a village in southeastern Poland ages ago (he claims to be a recent victim of his 89th birthday). Just short of age six he, a sister, and their parents arrived on what he calls *these shores* and settled in New Brunswick, New Jersey. At Rutgers he earned a B.A., M.A., and Ph.D. in English.

After a long and successful career in advertising and public relations, with adjunct teaching as a sideline, he retired in 1986 as director of public relations at the University of Rochester Medical Center. Since then he has authored a self-help book with a cancer survivor, published critiques of non-fiction material, and counseled other writers.

Puntification ~ No Pun Intended?

The late, great film director Alfred Hitchcock said (as I imagine the manner of his saying) in his deliberate, pontifical way, that the pun is "the highest form of humor." This is in contradistinction to the dictatorial declaration of Dr. Samuel Johnson, that the pun is the lowest form of humor.

My heart and mind are with Hitchcock.

There was once a man who, according to legend, entered a pun contest instigated by a local newspaper. He submitted ten entries, hoping that at least one would win, but to no avail: no pun in ten did.

Why is a pun usually greeted by rueful shakes of many heads and raucous groans? This reaction is common not to youths, but to groan-ups.

1

And why does virtually everyone preface a pun with "no pun intended," when it damned well is?

(cf. the other famous prefatory declaration 'meaning no disrespect') One could suppose that in both instances the subtext is something on the order of "I know, and you know, that what I'm about to say is outrageous, so please be kind and don't deride me for it."

At this juncture definitions may be useful. My Oxford English Dictionary (shorter version—only about 3700 pages, in two volumes) defines pun as the "humorous use of a word in such a way as to suggest two or more meanings, or of words with two different meanings—a play on words." My OED also defines pun as a variant of pound, as in making a substance firm by pounding it down. No fun there.

The Internet's *Wikipedia* weighs in with its characterization of the pun as "a figure of speech which consists of a deliberate confusion of similar words or phrases for rhetorical effect, whether humorous or serious."

Samuel Johnson's denunciation of puns is surprising, at least to us old English majors who expect him to enjoy manufacturing virtually any species of verbal playfulness. He could easily be expected, for example, to have a jokeular time toying with pun in his Dictionary, but not so; if anything, he seems almost overcome by ambivalence: "I know not whence this word is to be deduced; to pun is to grind or beat with a pestle; can pun mean an empty sound, like that of a mortar beaten, as clench, the old word for pun, seems only a corruption of clink? An equivocation; a quibble; an expression where a word has at once different meanings."

All this from a scholar who clearly had fun defining "network" as "anything reticulated or recussated, with interstices between the intersections." He was capable of wordplay. In his discussion of pun, on the other hand, he goes so far as to pass the baton to an earlier literary giant, Alexander Pope, who produced these lines:

> But fill their purse, the poet's work is done,
> Alike to them by patois or by pun.

Another giant of 18th-century English literature, playwright Richard Brinsley Sheridan, popularized a form of wordplay based on distorted use of words. Sheridan's fictional perpetrator of this folly was Mrs. Malaprop, a beloved comic character in Sheridan's play *The Rivals*. The silly lady donated her name to malapropism, defined by the OED as a "ludicrous misuse of words, especially in mistaking a word for another resembling it." This definition is not far removed from that of pun, with the principal difference residing in the deliberate wordplay that characterizes the pun, as opposed to the mistaken meanings that define malapropism.

A typical example of the latter in *The Rivals* has Mrs. Malaprop declare, "I would send her, at nine years old, to a boarding school—then, sir, she should have a supercilious knowledge in accounts, and as she grew up, I would have her instructed in geometry, that she might know something of the contagious countries; but above all, Sir Anthony, that she might not misspell and mispronounce words—this, Sir Anthony, is what I would have a woman know; and I don't think there is a superstitious article in it."

Those who prefer to simplify matters I refer to Walter Redfern. Author of *Puns* (Blackwell, London, 1984), who briefly defined pun as follows: "To pun

5

is to treat synonyms as homonyms."
To accept such an obscure simplifica-
tion is no fun; better to widen the
search for meaning, a procedure that
can lead to "paronomasia," a word of
Greek derivation that originally meant
calling something by a different name.
The Greeks apparently had a word for
it.

According to *Wikipedia*, puns can be
subdivided into a number of categories:

Homographic puns, which exploit dif-
ferences in meanings of words that
look, and often sound, alike, as in "Being in politics is like playing golf: you
can be trapped in one bad lie after
another."

Heteronymic puns, which are based on
words that   look alike but have different meanings as in, "What instrument
do fish play, bass guitar?"

Compound puns, which contain more than one pun, as for example in this one about a golf-cart shop in which there is a sign that reads, "When drinking, don't drive; don't even putt."

Extended puns, which tell a story containing multiple puns, as in this specimen: "A fight broke out in a restaurant kitchen. Egged on by waiters, two cooks peppered each other with punches. One of them, a foie gras specialist, ducked the first blows, but his goose was cooked when the other cold-cocked him. The man who thus beet his adversary, a weedy salad expert with cauliflower ears, tried to flee but was cornered in the maize of tables by an off duty cob. He was charged with a salt and batter-y."

As one might expect, puns come in other shapes, sizes, and categories (and languages), so numerous that they constitute a punderous mass. There are those who fear that most of them are too obscure or labored to be enjoyed, and such fears often outweigh the joy of scholarship.

You may be surprised to learn (I was) that the *Encyclopedia Britannica* takes a dim view of puns, which it seems to go out of its way to denigrate. As a particularly low example of the form the *Britannica* cites John Milton's reference to the prophet Elijah's ravens, which were, "though ravenous, taught to abstain from what they brought" (nothing, indeed, to crow about, but birds of a feather are what they are).

Also dismissed was Sigmund Freud's characterization of the Christmas season as "alcoholidays." As an example of higher, non-pun humor was a quotation from Groucho Marx, who said, "While on safari we shot two bucks, but that was all the money we had." (I would not want to coin such a phrase, either). It should have been obvious, especially to the *Britannica*, that Marx's quip is indeed a pun, however lame, by most definitions. It seems that when it suits its wishes, the *Britannica* does not hesitate to waive the rules (get it?).

It should be obvious that some brave souls engaged in the arts would employ puns to greater or lesser advantage. In this context the first name that comes to mind is Shakespeare, who turns puns into a kind of art form. When I think Shakespeare, I think "Hamlet," with particular reference to a bit of dialogue in Act IV, Scene iii. Hamlet has killed Polonius; not long after the fact the king enters, seeking Polonius:

King: "Now Hamlet, where's Polonius?"

Ham.: "At supper."

King: "At supper? Where?"

Ham.:   "Not where he eats, but where he is eaten; a certain convocation of politic worms are e'en at him. Your worm is your only emperor for diet."

The delightfully convoluted mind of Shakespeare is alive in these lines. The reference is to the so-called "Diet of Worms," a convocation ordered by the Holy Roman Emperor, who was seeking ways to overturn Martin Luther's revolution.

So there it all is: Diet (convocation); Worms (actually Wurms, the German city where the Diet was held); and Emperor ("politic" is a bonus, thrown in at no extra charge).

In Act III, Scene ii another sample of Shakespearean art unfolds: a troupe of actors has come to Elsinore in order to entertain the troops, (so to speak).

Hamlet and Polonius, patrons of the arts, discuss the matter:

Ham: "My lord, you played once i' the university, you say?"

Pol: "That I did, my lord, and was accounted a good actor."

Ham.: "And what did you enact?"

Pol.: "I did enact Julius Caesar; I was killed i' the Capitol; Brutus killed me."
Ham.: "It was a brute part of him to kill so capital a calf there."

The pervasiveness of puns is, and has been, such that puns (serious specimens, of course) occur in the Bible. In the New Testament (Matthew 16.18) Peter is told "Thou art Peter, and upon this rock I will build my church." In the original Greek text Peter is Petros, and "rock" is "Petra." Thus the pun. Or is it? After all, Jesus would have spoken to Peter (Simon at the time) in Aramaic, in which the man and the rock are "Cephas." There are scholars who believe that the passage was written by a speaker of Greek years after the death of Jesus. So go know.

Puns can be uttered spontaneously, without intent. For example, on a television newscast a man appeared who had been impaled on a ship's anchor. His injury was described as not life-threatening, but he did need surgery. Later, when the surgeon was asked how the operation went, the surgeon said, without thinking, "He sailed through it." In this instance, evidently, no pun was intended.

While punning is practiced in many languages, its acceptability varies with the cultural environment. Just as public belching is frowned upon in polite U.S. circles, in Mongolia it is a compliment to the chef. Therefore, puns, while they are considered a generic form of humor, they are in some parts of the U.S.

perceived as deceptive acts against listeners. Thus a pun can be delivered unexpectedly and in deadpan fashion and can be perceived at first as straight information. But it can become offensive when it is understood for what it really is. On the other hand, in the American South puns are often regarded as important rhetorical tools.

Despite the groans and wisecracks that are triggered by the mere mention of puns, a number of notables took them seriously enough to make known their views of the lowly art. Here are a few:

Fred Allen: Hanging is too good for the man who makes puns. He should be drawn and quoted.

Dave Barry: Puns are plays on words that a certain breed of person loves to spring on you and then look at you in a certain self-satisfied way.

Ambrose Bierce: A form of wit to which wise men stoop and fools aspire.

James Boswell: A good pun may be admitted among the smaller excellencies of lively conversation.

Samuel Taylor Coleridge: Punning may be the lowest but at all events may be the most harmless kind of wit because it never excites envy.

John Dryden: To torture one poor word ten thousand ways.

Henry Erskine on the pun as the lowest form of humor: It is, and therefore the foundation of all wit.

Oliver Wendell Holmes: People that make puns are like Wanton boys that put coppers on the railroad—but their little trick may upset a freight train of conversation for the sake of a battered witticism.

Samuel Johnson: If I were punished for every pun I shed, there would not be left a puny shed of my punish head.

Henry James: Blunt and I made atrocious puns. I believe, indeed, that Miss Blunt herself made a little punkin.

James Joyce: The pun is mightier than the sword.

Charles Lamb: A pistol let off at the ear, not a feather to tickle the intellect.

Oscar Levant: A pun is the lowest form of humor when you don't think of it first.

Edgar Allen Poe: Of puns it has been said that those who most dislike them are those who are the least able to utter them.

Jonathan Swift: A talent no man affects to despise but he that is without it.

Louis Untermeyer: Something every person belittles and everyone attempts.

With these learned historical and intellectual animadversions firmly in place, let us proceed to flesh out the meat of the matter in which we have a stake. What follows is a broad selection of puns, some original, others borrowed. Most are one-liners, i.e., brief definitions, comprising single words or short phrases:

PUNDAMENTALS
A Compundium preceded by a question, WHAT DO YOU CALL:

A law governing plagiarism? Statute of imitations.

A disease of the rich? Affluenza.

A state of unconsciousness caused by an eye condition? Glaucomatose.

A firearm displayed in a Tokyo theatre? Showgun.

A precise omelette? Eggsactly.

Moving two ten-cent pieces from one pocket to another? A pair-o'dimes shift.

Terminal illness? Airport disease.

Proof that Afghanistan has modern technology? Kabul TV.

A place where an ox preaches? A bully pulpit.

Pap smear? A paternity test.

A crappy adversary? An enema.

Burlesque queen whose boyfriend is a mobster? Strip moll.

Bacteria? Rear entrances to a cafeteria.

A mud puddle where ducks get stuck? Quackmire.

A cheesy boat race? A ricotta.

Punslinger? A gunman who shoots
from the quip.

Shamurai? Someone pretending to be a
Japanese warrior.

A mistake-prone. explosive CEO? A
blunderboss.

Conspiracy in a bedroom?

Chamberplot.

A young physician in charge of scan-
dalous behavior in a hospital?
A vice-resident.

Heifer loaf? A lazy young cow.

A sweet-tasting opportunistic photo
apparatus?   Candied camera.

Secretive visual observation?
Peek experience.

A comedian who tells short, abrupt
jokes? A curt jester.

Rapid transport of bushes with large
blossoms? Peony express.

Transport firm owned by a close
friend? Crony express.

Familiarity with strippers in sideshows?
Carnival knowledge.

A member of a women's religious order who is employed in Heaven?
Nun of the above.

A star of western movies who became
a bank officer? Loan ranger.

Last will and testament?
Dead giveaway.

Mouth-watering military organization?
Salivation Army.

An item of footwear that probes your
subconscious?
A Freudian slipper.

Three miles of intravenous tubing used
in Harvard Medical Center? I.V.
League.

A very well-dressed physical-fitness
trainer? Gym dandy.

A movie filmed in a nudist colony?

Skinema.

A nurse's unsuccessful effort to pierce a blood vessel? A vein attempt.

A shopping center devoted exclusively to headgear? Mart of the Hatter.

Potato pancakes served by King Arthur at the Round Table? Camelotkes

A funny documentary film? A jokeumentary.

A disease of the nouveau riche? Newmoneya.

A true film about a waterfowl? A duckumentary.

A true film about a rooster? A cockumentary.

A true film about a type of popular music? A rockumentary.

A true film about boxing? A sockumentary.

Surgical removal of wordplay?
A pundectomy.

An eccentric space traveler? Astronut.

A formal dance for domestic birds?
A fowl ball.

A sudden drop of an intestine?
A bowel fall.

A tennis player's earnings?
Net income.

Persistent illness of a musician?
The malady lingers on.

A noble woman who refuses to leave?
Milady lingers on.

A percussionist camel? A drumedary.

A soldier boy's best friend?
His mortar.

A devout Christian boy's best friend?
His martyr.

A hat with which to smash things?
Demolition derby.

A large ape that teaches Asian
philosophy? A gurulla.

Illumination for a marijuana party?
Potlight.

A nurse employed in a gastrointestinal
practice? A nurse-proctitioner.

COUNTRY MEDS

Benign: What you be after you be eight.

Barium: What to do with dead patients.

Caesarian section: A Roman neighborhood.

Catscan: A search for kitty.

Cauterize: Made eye contact with 'er.

Colic: My sheep dog has a bellyache.

Coma: A teeny punctuation mark.

BACK TO THE FARM

Where does a cattle rancher post instructions: On a bull-etin board.

What happens to a cow when she gives birth. She is decalfinated.

What do rookie stagecoach drivers learn? To hold their horses.

What is a favorite slogan for cattle? Every day is a hayday.

What do you call a cattle auction? A stock exchange.

What does a farmer call a dry cow? A milk dud.

How does a cow feel in mating season: Ready for a bull session.

BACK TO NORMAL

What do you call -

Dignified posture adopted by
proctologists? Rectitude.

A Rastafarian proctologist? Pokemon.

Someone who sprinkles his conversation with Yiddishisms? An oyster.

A major purchase that leaves the buyer
financially impotent? Cashtration.

A person who is a stupid asshole?
An ignoranus.

Euphoria at receiving a refund from
the I.R.S.? Intaxication.

After death, coming back to life as a
hillbilly? Reintarnation.

The gas cloud surrounding stupid people that stops ideas from penetrating? Bozone.

Misrepresenting yourself in order to impress a sex object? Foreploy.

High-up spray-painted drawings and messages? Giraffiti.

The gulf between sarcastic wit and the person who fails to get it? Sarchasm

Taking coffee intravenously? Inoculatte.

A degenerate disease? Osteopornosis.

Hosts of bad vibes leading to the apocalypse? Karmageddon.

Getting work done while drinking only emasculated beverages? Decafalon.

All talk and no action? Glibido.

The tendency of stupid ideas to fly past
you and recede into the distance?
Dopeler effect.

The frantic dance you do after being
bitten by a spider? Arachnoleptic fit.

Satan in the form of a persistent mos-
quito? Beelzebug.

The color you turn when you find half
a worm in your apple? Caterpallor.

The person on whom you cough?
Coffee.

Appalled by weight gain?
Flabbergasted.

Giving up hope of having a powerful
upper body? Absdicate.

Attempting an explanation while
drunk? Esplanade.

Impotent? Willy-nilly.

Answering the door while wearing a
see-through robe? Negligent.

Walking with a lisp? Lymph.

Olive-flavored mouthwash? Gargoil.

An emergency vehicle picking up
someone who has been run over by a
steamroller? A flatulence.

A rapidly receding hairline?

Balderdash.

PUNDEROUS WIT

I

While the funeral service was taking place in the chapel, the driver of the hearse was passing the time in idle conversation with the off-duty motorcycle policeman who would be guiding the cortege to the cemetery.

"I should think," said Pilesser, the policeman, "that your profession might, in its incessant focus on intimations of immortality, induce a potentially burdensome level of psychic stress."

The hearse driver, Gansevoort, looked thoughtful. "Intimations of mortality, more likely," he responded. "Actually, in the course of time, I have been able to prevent stress by concentrating on the philosophical implications of my job."

"Are you thinking in existential terms?" Pilesser inquired.

"Not really," said the other. "For me, Descartes is more relevant."

"For example?"

"For example, Descartes sees the ultimate rationalist taking a mechanistic view of matter, explaining it in corpuscular terms, He held that we are all machines, except for the spirit."

"And this," Pilesser said admiringly, "impacts your stress level in a positive way?" Gansevoort nodded.

"Well, then," Pilesser continued, "you wouldn't mind augmenting my comprehension of Cartesian concepts right at this time. Even if it means a slight delay in the proceedings for which we are here?"

Gansevoort shook his head. "I'm sorry," he allowed, "but that would be putting Descartes before the hearse."

II

Rotenturm had just returned home after a visit to his gastroenterologist. It was the third visit in two weeks. He was in obvious distress. Sensing the state of his emotions, his wife quietly took him by the hand, led him to the sofa in the den, and sat down by his side. "What is it?" she inquired gently.

"My goddam gut is doing nip ups," Rotenturm hissed between clenched teeth. "First it's stopped up like a plugged-up drain. So after a few days of that bloody mess, I go to my G.I. man. So what does he do?"

"Let me guess," said the wife. "He said to try roughage, like the good minimalist he is."

"Exactly," Rotenturm spat out. "I go with the fruit-and-vegetables routine, and nothing happens. So the second time around, the eminent specialist says I'd better get some enemas. I told him I hate messing with those gizmos, and how about some pills? He says, 'all right, give it a shot,' and he handed me some samples."

"And did the pills work?" asked the missus.

"Not all the way, but the old drainpipe is trending that way. Yeah, definitely trending. So I called his G.I. nibs and told him."

"And was he pleased?"

"Oh, for sure. What he said was, 'With trends like these, who needs enemas?' "

III

After an unusually dry spring and an abnormally wet summer, the harvest was estimated to be barely enough to sustain the village population through the fall and winter. This posed an unprecedented dilemma for the village elders.

On the one hand, the population had a long- honored tradition of celebrating the harvest, which had been abundant for several generations, with a fete, an event to which everyone looked forward with keen anticipation. On the other hand, a fete celebrated in the face of certain scarcity to come would surely have serious repercussions.

This dilemma set the tone of the discussion at the annual fall meeting of the village Council of Elders. Kleinhans, the youngest member of the group, opened the meeting by arguing that the fete should be held. "The people expect it," he declared. "To cancel it would only pile woe upon woe."

"I take your point," said Balmundo, "and I am tempted to go along with your recommendation. But the way I see it, a fete at this point in time would have the effect of calling unwanted attention to the calamity that we face."

Gangliaux disagreed. "I favor holding the fete precisely because we face a difficult time. The people's morale needs a positive stimulus at a time like this."

"There's an aspect of this matter that no one has touched upon," Himmelfarb interposed. "How can we use any part of our slim stock of food for a party when there's barely enough to avert starvation?"

The Council members looked anxiously at one another and then turned to Rechschafer, the chief elder, who was looking thoughtfully at the ceiling. After a tense silence he spoke.

"I am quite firm in my conviction that a traditional fete is out of the question. Gangliaux's suggestion that a fete be held for morale considerations makes sense and I am tempted to favor it. But on further analysis of all the factors involved, I must say that to do it would lead to a fete worse than dearth."

IV

A NASA rocket scientist arrives at the offices of a firm that specializes in launching spacecraft. He is ushered into the office of a corporate executive, to whom he introduces himself and tells a sad tale: "We have a vital mission ready to go but sir, as you know, the government is phasing out of rocketry. So I want to know what it would cost to launch our rocket."

"Just offhand," said the executive, "I would guess about twenty-five million. That's about average."

The rocket man shook his head. "No way we're going to get more than a small fraction of that from the budget. Tell you what: if you do it without charge, you're sure to get more than the figure you name in free publicity. How about it?"

The executive rose to his feet and shaking his head, he declared, don't you know there's no such thing as a free launch?"

PUN 'N GAMES

A Duelogue

At this p oint I offer, at no extra charge or obligation, a word game that two can play, a pun-on-pun that can lead to a happy blending. The players agree on a subject and on who may strike the first blow. They then take turns pelting each other with quips that, rather than passing in the night, play variations on the scheme. Suppose, for example, that the subject is electricity:

A. Wire you bothering me?

B. Because I get a charge out of it.

A. Can't we discuss current events?

B. I'll volt for that.

A. Ohm my! This is a joule of an idea.

Indeed, it can be electrifying—and so on into the night, until one player has exhausted his or her possibilities and admits the utility of surrender. So switch on the ingenuity and have pun.

NOW SOME BONUS PUNTS

The roundest knight at King Arthur's table was Sir Cumference.

I thought I saw an eye doctor on an Alaskan island, but it turned out to be an optical Aleutian.

She was only a Kentucky whiskey
maker, but he gave proof that he loved
her still.

A rubber-band pistol was confiscated
in algebra class because it was a weapon
of math disruption.

No matter how hard you push the
envelope, it continues to remain
stationary.

A dog gave birth to puppies in a public
park and was ticketed for littering.

Two silkworms had a race, which
ended in a tie.

A grenade thrown into a kitchen in
France would result in Linoleum
Blownapart.

A hole has been found in the wall of a
nudist camp; the police are looking
into it.

An atheists' club is a non-prophet organization.

Two hats were hanging on a hatrack. One said, "You stay here. I'll go on a head."

I wondered why the baseball with which I was playing was getting bigger. Then it hit me.

A sign on the lawn of a drug rehab center said, "Keep off the grass."

The short psychic who escaped from prison was a medium at large.

The man who escaped from mustard gas and pepper spray is now a seasoned veteran.

In democracy it's your vote that counts. In feudalism it's your count that votes.

A backward poet writes inverse.

AND FINALLY (this one is very naughty, so feel free to skip it)

I know a computer nerd who calls his genitals his hard drive.

P.S. What do you call obscene, vulgar sexual activity: Pornication.

Now, dear reader, this space is reserved for your own private mental punishment. Grab your puncil or puntbrush and join the puntocracy:

_____

_____

_____

_____

_____

_____

_____

_____

_____

_____

_____

_____

_____

_____

_____

_____

_____

_____